GOLDEN RATIO IN UX DESIGN

AND OTHER ARTICLES ON USER EXPERIENCE

AMOLENDU H.

XpressPublishing
An imprint of Notion Press

XpressPublishing
An imprint of Notion Press

No.8, 3rd Cross Street,CIT Colony,
Mylapore, Chennai, Tamil Nadu-600004

ISBN 978-1-64983-070-8

To my wife Moumita, who is one of the best UX designers
I know of, and the inspiration behind this book.

Contents

1. Golden Ratio In Ux Design   1

2. Ux Research – Why Is It Necessary?   11

3. Psychological Principles In User Experience   20

4. Role Of Analytics In Ux   27

5. Dark Patterns – Is It Ethical?   35

6. Natural User Experience   42

7. Mind Mapping In Ux Design   50

8. Why Should A Tech Start-up Get Their Product Designs Done From A Ux Agency?   57

9. Designing For The "gen-z"   63

10. How Users Get Motivated Towards using Some Apps Due To The Disastrous Situation?   69

11. The Ux Design Trends – 2010-2020   75

12. Customer Experience Trends 2020   82

Thank You   89

CHAPTER I

Golden Ratio in UX Design

Leonardo Fibonacci and the Golden Ratio

Designs need to be in sync with proportions. Offline designs are based on design principles that are standards and accepted worldwide, however, UX and especially UI designers have also to a greater extent been using design principles that rule the offline designs. The design aesthetics are not created randomly but are designed under the purview of calculated measures and rules. In addition to taking care of the other aspects of designing like usability, user-centric designs, technology, validated designs, and unparalleled experiences, it is also important to maintain a consistency of design and proportions. In defining this, two major design principles come to aid, the Golden Ratio and the Fibonacci Sequence.

While Golden Ratio and Fibonacci Sequence draw inspiration from nature, they have been used since aeons for creating architectural structures including the pyramids of Egypt. Now, what is the resemblance between an offline design and an online one, and how these design principles can come to rescue UX designers? Let us explore in this blog.

The principles we discuss here are mathematical expressions and has been adapted in music, painting, architecture, nature, and photography. UX designers have also gone ahead and adapted to these design principles to develop their own specialty.

Golden Ratio

The golden ratio is defined as 1:1.618 and represented by the Greek symbol Phi. The mathematical expression of the ratio is represented as A/B = (A+B)/A = 1.618. The figure is often rounded to the 1.162 for greater ease in calculations.

The simplest expression of the golden ratio is, if one side of a figure, say the length 'A' is 100px, then its width 'B' by default would be 1.1618px.

$$\frac{A}{B} = \frac{A + B}{A} = 1.618...$$

A + B	
A	B

The golden ratio formula shows that length A is 1.618 times the length B. You can validate if two lengths follow the ratio by dividing their lengths.

The Golden ratio is very astutely crafted around inspiration from nature. This ratio is also related to a sequence of consecutive numbers that are known as the Fibonacci Sequence, which is again inspired by nature. From the shape of a shell to the whorl of leaves, the placement of petals all is nature's way of the Fibonacci Sequence. It gets the name from its observer Fibonacci, an Italian Mathematician. Fibonacci came with a series of numbers where the earlier two numbers sum up to the next number. The Fibonacci Sequence of numbers is – 0,1,1,2,3,5,8,13...

This sequence is adapted in building a spiral to define the aesthetics of the design and placement of elements in the design. Let us see this very interesting way, how the Fibonacci Sequence is used to create a spiral.

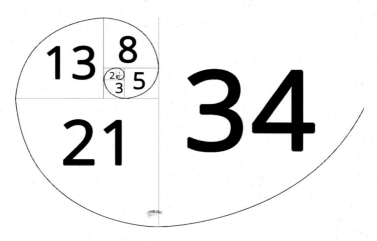

Creating the Fibonacci Spiral

How Fibonacci and the Golden Ratio are related?

The ratio of adjacent numbers in a Fibonacci sequence is close encounters to 1.16 which is the Golden Ratio. Let us see how in the image below:

A	B	B / A
2	3	1.5
3	5	1.666666666...
5	8	1.6
8	13	1.625
...	...	...
144	233	1.618055556...
233	377	1.618025751...
...	...	...

Fibonacci and the Golden Ratio

Applicability in UX designs

Fibonacci and Golden Ratio have been applied across your UX designs in a variety of ways to create captivating design experiences.

Font

The golden ratio can be used to determine the font size for a web page or Mobile App. With a little math, determining the aspect ratio will be easier. If you wish to consider a font size of 11 for your body text, the text size for the heading can be 11px X 1.1618 = 12.7px which can be rounded to 13px.

Image Cropping

Placing the golden spiral on an image can give the exact aspect ratio for cropping an image. Looking at the example below, we know the portion of the image we want to retain and which to crop. This is also known as the rule of thirds in the photography terminology.

Image Cropping – Rule of Thirds, Source: Digital Photograph School

Layout

The Golden Ratio proportion helps create a compelling and visually appealing display.

The golden ratio can ascertain a visually good composition.

It can maintain the design aesthetics without deviating from the visual hierarchy of placing different components in a design.

For a sense of creating powerful typography in design, the designers need to make use of aspect ratio that can be calculated by the golden ratio rule. The typography can be for headers, sub-headers, and body. These typographical measurements can be well calculated with the golden ratio.

The use of white spaces in a design can be well crafted around your golden ratio, just that the design seems impeccably right flaunting your whites.

A sense of proportion and harmony is established ensuring good first impressions as well as visceral reaction (the sense of concluding a design within a matter of seconds).

Golden Ratio in nature

Golden Ratio is exclusively seen in nature from the flower whorls to the placement of leaves, shells formations, etc. What more inspiration can one draw when nature itself exhibits the golden ratio.

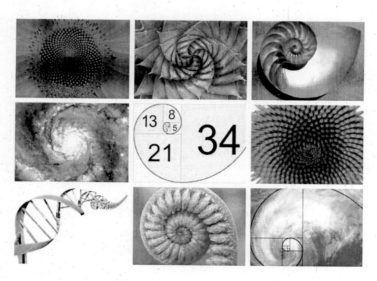

Fibonacci Spiral in Nature, Source:
Educateinspirechange.Org

Golden Ratio in Logos

Logos are a design packed representation of your brand and the golden ratio can aid in creating some sophisticated and simplistic logo designs.

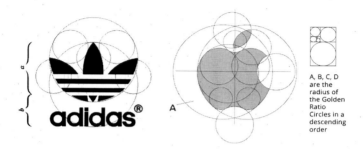

A, B, C, D are the radius of the Golden Ratio Circles in a descending order

Adidas logo was designed by Adi Dassler and Apple logo was designed by Rob Janoff

Golden ration in Mobile Apps

Mobile apps offer lesser space and therefore need to be impactful. Creating designs that can call for immediate action are not just aesthetically built, but proportionately right. Having the Golden Rectangle placed over your design layout will help determine where the necessary action triggers need to be incorporated in the design. Like the save to favorites or buy this product, or move to cart action triggers can be placed at the innermost whorl of the curve.

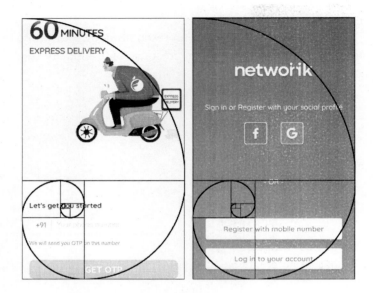

Our design team followed the golden ratio while designing some recent apps for ur clients Fraazo and Networrk

Golden ratio in websites

The website allows a lot of play areas for practicing the golden ratio. Designers can use the golden ratio to generate proportions and designs that look simple yet elegant.

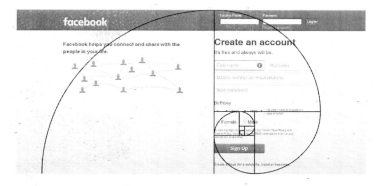

Facebook log in page

Automated Golden Ratio Calculator

Various widgets and apps give you the freedom of calculating automated measurements. Some of the known ones are Omni Calculator, MiniWebTool. Applications are specifically used for calculating the golden ratio of a face. For e.g. WPCalc, Golden Ratio Face, CalcalCulatorSoup, etc.

Golden Ratio comes to assorted components of a design in a perfect placement that is visually pleasing, aesthetically correct as well as functionally right. Having the right elements on the page can be worked around a simple formula, which might look intimidating, but, is simple math that nature too represents.

The golden ratio has been used for ages in different streams of art including architecture, sculpture, photography. However, designers have adapted this ratio to the online design platform has created some overwhelming designs that bring a sense of harmony and balance. Knowing the first impressions create a tremendous effect, the golden ratio has been adopted universally for creating impressive designs.

CHAPTER II

UX Research – Why Is It Necessary?

The USA Interviews conducted research on why companies and teams conducted research across various industries, job requirements, and geographies. Their projections and analysis largely cover the underlying importance of research across different domains and the result is a product/solution that is well accepted on release. The core findings on a scale of 7, where 7 depicts the highest importance, states the value of research.

The projected results show the maximum research result is the engagement with customers to understand the customer's need, followed by validating the prototypes to build better products or solutions.

> "*The only source of competitive advantage is the one that can survive technology fuelled disruption — an obsession with understanding, delighting, connecting with, and serving customers. In this age, companies that thrive are those that tilt their budgets toward customer knowledge and relationships.*"

- Laura Kein, the author of UX Lean Start-ups & Build Better Products states

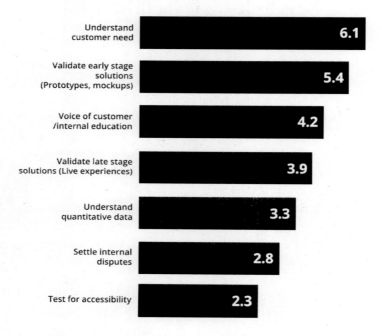

What is most important goal of your research program?

Goal	Value
Understand customer need	6.1
Validate early stage solutions (Prototypes, mockups)	5.4
Voice of customer /internal education	4.2
Validate late stage solutions (Live experiences)	3.9
Understand quantitative data	3.3
Settle internal disputes	2.8
Test for accessibility	2.3

User Interviews - Average (1-7 scale, a bigger number means more important)

Research is a fundamental step in the designing process. Rather the initial one, that builds the very foundation of design.

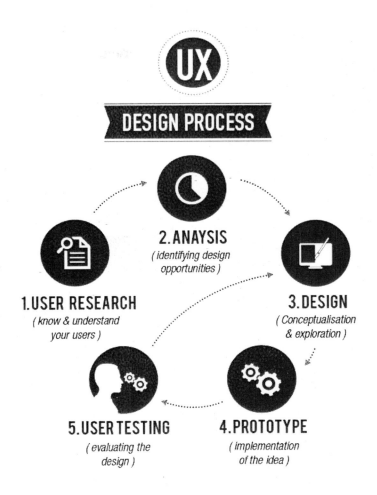

UX Design Process

The imperative need to build design is supplemented by research. If designers are merely building solutions across the inputs from the client in the name of cost & sustainability, it will result is a run-of-the-mill product, a boxed product that was replicated or could be replicated. The core of UX design is research. If research is not substantially done, the result will be a blotched-up process ahead as well as a hike in maintenance cost for salvaging the project.

Fundamentals of UX design

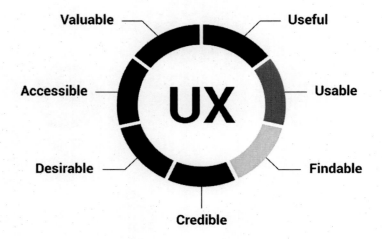

Image source: Interaction-Design.Org

UX design is built around the fundamentals of the wheel above. The different parameters in varied proportions make for a successful product. But then, how does one arrive at a unique solution is by engaging in research around these parameters. Trends don't make a design acceptable, but its usability and usability is defined by the consumers.

Your Strategy for Research

Designers have been toying with different research instruments to derive qualitative as well as quantitative results. The time and cost factors are often the reasons that clients want to eliminate these two processes totally. The designers are then left lurking with the challenge of designing by replicating existing designs or a sub-standard solution that will not come to benefit the end-user. The end-user is not the designer or the client. The end-user needs are different and varied and need to be decoded to a satisfying solution.

An end-user can effectively substantiate the gap between the client's demand and the designer's creative reach by providing real type data.

Broadly classified research is done in two formats

- Generative: Research on a set of consumers and a specific problem area.
- Evaluative: Research that is done on a design or a concept.

Research methodologies for the UX design can be classified as

Lean UX: Lean UX Research works on hypothesis, where a prototype is built and then user research is done around the prototype. This is a cost-saving measure.

Guerrilla Research: Guerrilla Research is a random research methodology used in UX design research. The research entails a small chunk of users and evaluates certain design elements. Because of its narrow approach, it can be a cost-saving practice, but not holistically rewarding.

Heuristic Evaluation: Heuristic Research and evaluation make use of the best practices and guidelines to arrive at analysis or decisions. This method can be used to eliminate future project lags and loopholes.

Building Hypothetical Personas:
Creating hypothetical personas of your consumer on the basis of the data presented by the client. In situations where user research is not possible due to time or money constraints, hypothetical personas can be built on assumptions.

Brainstorming: Brainstorming is again based on data that is available from the research or an off-hand data that the client has presented. Brainstorming is again within the team and might fail to bring the consumer's perspective to the design.

Minimum Viable Research: Minimum viable research is conducting research as much that it supplements the purpose of the project requirement. This means a cost-efficient measure.

Subject Matter Expert Interviews

This methodology makes use of subject matter expert advice and works around the directives shared by the expert. The expert works on the problem areas and offers analysis and solutions. This practice can bring a deeper level of understanding of the topic of research, yet a little shy of the consumer experience.

UX research eliminates assumptions, offers real-time data, brings a realistic outlook to prototyping, avoids design duplication or standardization, offers scope to explore designs.

Skipping research will show its repercussions in the formative stages when the possibility of change means more time and money investment, delay in schedules, and at the end of it the distress when the consumer does not accept the solution as they cannot relate.

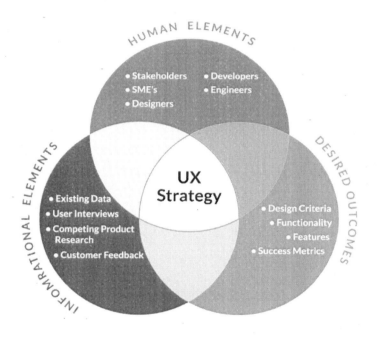

Illustration by Sherif Amin

Research is a fulfilling experience because they result in:

- User-centric designs

- Target – user-specific solutions
- Target product usability and efficiency
- Understand customer pain points
- Helps build better workflow assessment and design prototype
- Eliminates future errors in the project
- Eliminates possible spiked-up project costs
- Successful goal achievement
- Well-accepted and efficient designs
- Lesser customer support calls
- Enhanced revenues
- Accelerated development at no extra cost

Quantifying on the Return on Investment

Often every client focuses on the return on investment, and as a designer to be able to convince a client that good research will certainly quantify to a good return on investment. Because then, you are making a bespoke product that purely answers the consumer queries and refines their experience.

The designer should involve all the stakeholders in the project and make them well aware of the value of research and future payoffs. The designer should be able to bring forth the project projection that not only is conveying of the technicalities, but the need for research to create an authentic and unique product.

> "In a recent UserTesting study, 36% of companies reported that their UX budget had increased since last year, and 27% said that the increase was due to a change in attitude towards user research."

- UserTesting.com

It is an undeniable truth that UX research is not optional, but an important process that builds up to unique experiences.

CHAPTER III

Psychological Principles in User Experience

Design emote in their ways, communicate, and call for a reaction from the consumers. This could be a closed sale or a consumer shifting to a competitor site. User Experience is defined around various design experiences. The design platform is vast, considering creating experiences that can run beyond the scope of application. To make design a standard, relatable and definite experience, certain psychology principles are derived that designers should abide by.

In light of these design psychology principles, designs can be decoded to create experiences that can be applied and interpreted as norms. Creating in the framework of design psychology helps to connect to clients as well as consumers equally and they understand the relevance of design output. There are numerous design principles, but the more ubiquitous are listed here.

Hick's Law

The more the merrier does not apply under Hick's law. Hick's law is about taking a conservative and decluttered approach to make design simple and hence actionable. According to the law, the more the options you present to your consumers, the more time they take to decide.

Sites with minimalist designs appear promising, but how about their usability? What about sites that are heavy on content, how are those aligned and captured under Hick's law? It is the designer's skill to chunk and navigates the options under a smart infrastructure architecture, yet make the design appear simple and purposeful.

Psychology of Persuasion

Psychology of Persuasion very strongly and aptly captures the consumer responses bringing them to a call for action. The triggers introduced by persuasion are intriguingly response-oriented and therefore adapted by many designers.

Reciprocity:
Reciprocity is creating indebtedness such that the consumer is obliged and comes back to shop. E.g. – Offers and free vouchers.

Authority:
Authority is making use of authoritative figures or celebrity endorsements to capture consumer interest.

Scarcity:
Creating a deprived environment, which in turn triggers consumers to act fast. Timed sales, limited offers, stock clearances all work around the scarcity law.

Psychology of Colours:
What are you looking forth to drive? What is your purpose behind the design? Who is your target audience and what are their buying behavioural patterns? As a brand what do you wish to communicate to your audience?

Colours come to influence the design and inspire a call to action. The deep and interesting psychology of colours can be adapted to convey brand value or to trigger sales.

- RED: Love, Passion, Energy, Power, Strength
- ORANGE: Courage, Confidence, Friendliness, Success

- YELLOW: Energy, Warmness, Happiness, Joyfulness
- GREEN: Environment, New, Money, Fertility, Earth, Healing, Freshness
- BLUE: Calming, Peaceful, Divine, Professional, Trusting, Traditional
- PURPLE: Royalty, Spirituality, Ambition, Wealth, Luxury
- BLACK: Classy, Protection, Elegance, Formality

Corporates bank on the blue colour symbolising professionalism and trust. Luxury and high-end products make the use of purple; while bold brands make their statement with Black.

Colours are also intelligently placed to create a call for action. Different colours have different impacts on the individual mind and help trigger or curtail actions.

Psychology of Shapes:

Psychology of Shapes, Source Daniellevanstee.Com

Like Colours, our subconscious mind also reacts to different shapes by relating different qualities to different shapes. These are usually memory-based visual interpretations that we associate with certain qualities and have deep-set in our minds.

Designers make use of colour and shape to create visually compelling designs that engage and impact.

Gestalt Principles of Visual Perception

The Gestalt principle of perception states that elements placed together are perceived as one. The Gestalt Principle is narrowly classified under different principles:

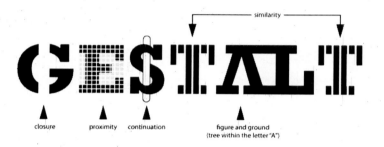

GESTALT Principles

Law of Symmetry:
This design aspect uses symmetry in design to capture user experience.

Law of Proximity:
Elements, when placed in closed proximity, gives the appearance of a design that is bold and captivating.

Law of Similarity:
Similar objects when placed in closed proximity offer a united feel and this enhances the design in a certain dimension.

Law of Continuity:
This law establishes a connection from one object in a

design to another under a smooth and unaltered flow. Often represented by curved lines.

Law of Closure:

Law of the closure means an incomplete object that is designed to perceive as complete.

Figure & Ground:

This is a captivating representation of design where one image can be perceived in different forms.

Above logo by Logoworks is made as per the Figure & Ground law, where the butterfly wings also come to represent two human side faces.

Visceral Reactions:

Why do you keep coming back to a shopping website often? Is it the product range or the product display, the ease of access, the convenience of controls? These all factors add to comforting results and hence you would want to get back to these sites often as compared to others. This is the visceral reaction of the website to you. Visceral reactions are a stimulus to designs and keep consumers coming back to your designs.

Visceral reactions are highly creative and impactful designs that are explicitly built across user experiences.

The elaborate elements like imagery, fonts, colours, and graphic are used to enhance the design.

Von Restorff Effect

The selective distinction is the way the Von Restorff Effect works breaking the monotony. It is also known as Isolation effect.

The design stands by making a visual distinction of an object such that it stands stark in contrast to the others making a memorable experience.

This effect is created by working artistically around highlighting, altering colours, size, font, or effect of the object that has to be distinguished to a call-to-action.

Screenshot from Evernote.Com plans page, the "Sign-Up" and "Free Trial" buttons are actually Green while rest of the pages are greyscaled

Von Restorff effect is usually seen in the call to action buttons that sit stark contrasting to the other elements in the design. In the above image subtly, the Von Restorff effect is the Free tab as opposed to the other two paid ones.

There are innumerable principles of design psychology including – Dual Coding Theory, Pareto Principle, Fitt's Law, Mental Models, Memory Models, Memory

Limitations, Selective Disregards, and Change Blindness, Cognitive Load, Serial Position Effect, etc. It is, after all, a choice of the designer to adapt to a principle that is befitting the consumer and stakeholder demands as well as can trigger a suitable call-for-action. While psychology principles of design help maintain a standard across the industry, it is also easy to make understand the stakeholders of the design element and expected results. These design principles are based around consumer decisions and design expectations and therefore drive towards effectively meeting the goals.

CHAPTER IV

Role of Analytics in UX

How often have you seen a website that has captured your attention, and has been an exclusive design experience? When I say design experience, a layman should also enjoy surfing the website and should find an easy way to affect a task, he /she is on while visiting the site. A website that is bringing a full-fledged experience is certainly a result of good planning, design, executions, and also a feedback process. The feedback process is a fuel system that runs the entire process and makes it enriching for the consumers. The feedback process can also be alternated as research, of knowing what the consumers are seeking. In the digital arena, research and findings are attributed to analytics, the science of real-time data and analysis.

While UX designers are aiming towards presenting best design experiences, the ideal and unique designs are only a result of analytics, of understanding consumer behaviour patterns and designing around their experiences.

Analytics is the measurement of consumer activity on a website or an app during a certain period of time documented and used for critical analysis to draw conclusions and projections.

Analytics are conducted to

- Designing user-data backed experiences.
- To understand user behavioural patterns towards designs and expectations.
- Data-backed re-designing of visual patterns based on usability.

- Designing as per need and not as per the principles of designing.
- Gap user experiences towards an uninterrupted experience.
- Enhance conversions through the site.

Analytics are primarily classified as Qualitative and Quantitative. Whatever aspect of your design or business you want to focus on will come under these two broad categories.

But let us understand what Qualitative and Quantitative analytics mean.

Qualitative:

Qualitative analytics are inclined towards the why of the situation. They are conducted to understand a visible gap, newer insights, testing existing designs, and capturing consumer behaviours.

Quantitative:

Quantitative Analytics is inclined towards capturing statistical data, and number crunchers.

Your Need

Depending on your specific need a particular analytical method can be adopted and in a particular scenario, a mix of both analytical methods can be consolidated. The choice of method is also driven by your test parameters and your budget.

What do you plan to assess?

- What is the overall impact of an existing design or the one you are building on?

- What is the expected change? Where is the change expected?
- Inputs on your existing features or new features?
- Are you checking on consumer traffic and revisits?
- Do you plan to assess your goal conversion?
- User Error Frequency
- Customer Satisfaction
- Visitors who purchased and the ones who quit

Analytical tools are handy and offer to gather real-time data. These tools will require time investment as well as money. The idea is to specifically design your requirement, set parameters for analysis such that you save time as well as constrict on the money spend.

Analytics are also adopted to infer:

Descriptive:
Descriptive analysis help derives data as a number of clicks, videos viewed, and site visits.

Diagnostic:
The diagnostic analysis is devised on the same parameters as descriptive, but questions the qualitative aspects, as asking Why? It ascertains why a certain aspect of the business is not functioning as per expectations and what are the possible loopholes that can be gapped.

Prescriptive:
The prescriptive analysis is about how the loopholes can be gapped. They offer solutions to existing issues.

Predictive:
The Predictive analysis is a pro-active indicator of ascertaining the future of design, product, or process. It analyses the current data of the shortcomings and the

duality of things and presents an evaluation of the situation, making things easier for you to decide.

The Application of Analytics

Merely conducting analytics and measuring qualitative and quantitative results does not mean a solution, but just an indication of what needs to be achieved. The process might require constant analysis of the parameters set until the design is finalised.

The Tools for Analytics

User Session Recording:
This process practices recordings of the user sessions, which offer a step by step user interaction details of the consumer with the websites/app. Capturing the user journey experience makes analysis and understanding of the issues on the website/app real-time data to work on.

Touch Heatmaps:
Touch heatmaps capture the most accessed area on the website/app showcasing the usual operative pattern of the consumers. This app captures well the taps, double taps, swipes and other touch gestures on the screen to deduce information.

 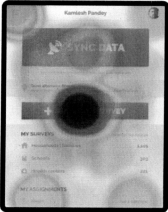

Touch heatmaps analysis, the darker shade denotes more numbers

This data is then presented in the form of captivating heatmaps on the app itself, to show the user activity around the specific usability and design parameters. The heat maps are colour-coded ranging from Blue to Red. Red represents intense activity on the continuum, whereas, blue represents the least activity.

User Flow Maps:
User flow maps guide by capturing data on the user's journey on the site before making a purchase or logging out without a purchase.

Real-time Analytics:
Realtime analytics offers data on the current live scenario as well as how many users are currently on your site or browsing on a certain page.

Website Usage Analysis:
Website Usage Analytics is used to understand:

- Which content is trending and which does not make much difference?
- The reason for the loss of consumers to competitors.
- Monitoring certain campaigns.

There are loads of paid and free apps that can lead to your desired analysis. Google Analytics is a widely used free web analytics. However, a paid version offers an exhaustive service portfolio.

Eye Tracking Analysis:

The one tool that obeys no physical interference, yet, captures data is the Eye Tracking Device. It cleverly captures where the consumer's vision moves across the screen and what aspect of the website /app is more accessed or seen and the duration. Eye Tracking Device is a sensory technique and captures the focus and attention of a consumer across versatile devices. It actually helps understand the behaviour and decision-making patterns of consumers helping refine design experiences.

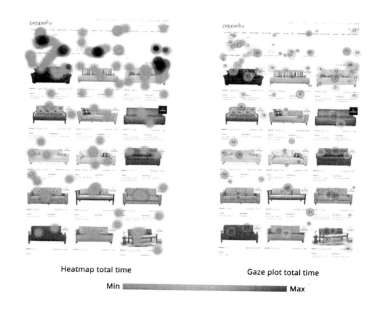

Heatmap total time   Gaze plot total time

Min ▬▬▬▬▬▬▬▬▬▬▬▬▬▬ Max

Key Insights: from 2016 Pepperfry UX Research, in the Sofa Selection Page: The gaze plot shows that the user is confirming the selection of the type of sofa. i.e. three-seaters, two-seaters, or single-seater. All the options visible on the page are looked at least once. The designs and colours determine the movement of the eye as the gaze plot shows the eye movement is not linear or any particular pattern. We also found the user looks on the first 3-4 rows and the last 3-4 rows on the page for more time , so it's recommended to place your more targetted items. Note: the darker shade denotes more numbers.

Attention span, length of duration of visit, movement of the eye, focus areas and unseen areas on the screen come to depict a lot about consumer behaviour. Intense activity around a product shows it is much liked or ready to be bought, the scattered vision around the screen shows a curiosity for skimming through other possible options, the distribution of intense activity on a site shows interesting or eye-catching content, etc. There are various insights that you can draw on consumer activities, but sure enough, real-time data can be obtained through this unique and acutely natural tool.

Too much data will be a feed but not a solution. The extent of data that you have captured, how relevant is it to your requirement? Have your metrics been defined accurately to capture the right data? Is your data-oriented towards a larger picture and not towards a specific attribute you wish to capture? You can swim in an ocean of data and yet come out thirsty. The quest is to make justice to your time, efforts, and money invested in analytics. Analytics can fetch you loads of real-time but the processing and interpretation are the work of an analytics expert. An analytics expert can bridge the gap between data and projections and make the entire process worth the effort.

CHAPTER V

Dark Patterns – Is It Ethical?

What drives us to some e-commerce shopping sites often? Firstly, due credits to access the plethora of products under one domain, and the presentability. Secondly, something we all can't deny is comfort and pricing, you do not get all year around "Sale" in the offline world. Thirdly, the site functionality and the loading time. The consumers are unaware of deep design elements and labyrinth of patterns that designers have created to offer easy and accessible designs. What happens in the backend is a sinkhole that traps consumers unawares.

The pattern of usability is the efficiency with which the user can access sites. However, in creating client experiences designers have gone way ahead creating patterns that are undisputedly efficient and result-oriented but a tangled web called dark patterns.

Most of the time you will not be aware of the farce the companies are creating to keep you coming back. User experience does bring the comfort of easy access, but stealthily extracts information or psychologically manipulates consumers to act even in unwanted situations.

Darkpatterns.Org very plainly explains dark patterns as tricks used in websites and apps that make you do things that you didn't mean to, like buying or signing up for something. This site is created to spread the awareness of dark patterns and how they come to influence consumers and shame companies.

Types of Dark Patterns

A dark pattern is a maze and is classified under various types. We all have experienced some of the other dark patterns while surfing online. However, the intensity and ethical pursuit of these dark patterns remain a huge question. There are numerous types of dark pattern, but we have listed a handful here-

Disguised Ads

Disguised ads are plentiful on e-commerce websites, tricking us with colours and patterns and unexpected buttons on the payments page, which till then did not just exist. Often these triggers are set sitting adjacent to the action button, like include insurance, donate for charity, etc. Often in the maze of designs companies make you take decisions that you never wanted.

Scarcity

Human minds are programmed to act fast in scarcity mode and the action trigger is procuring the item before it is out of stock. That might just not happen as this is a tactic crafted to sell, and you end up buying.

The utter disgrace could be, the companies have so well accepted and adopted to the dark patterns that in critical conditions to they keep playing their usual marketing gimmick.

While e-commerce sites are listing their service unavailability during the COVID-19 worldwide lockdowns, a well-known hotel booking site, continues to lure us with the scarcity pattern.

Room Type	Sleeps	Price for 2 nights	Your Choices	Select Rooms	
Double Room 1 king bed	👥👥	₹ 8,500 +₹ 1,020 taxes and charges	🍽 Continental breakfast ❓ included ✓ **Partially refundable** Only 3 rooms left on our site **Dark Pattern**	0 ▾	**I'll reserve** • It only takes 2 minutes • Confirmation is immediate • No booking or credit card fees!

26 m² ❄ Air conditioning
Private Bathroom
Flat-screen TV

✓ Free toiletries   ✓ Toilet
✓ Bathtub or shower   ✓ Towels
✓ Linens   ✓ Cleaning products
✓ Tile/Marble floor   ✓ Desk
✓ Private entrance   ✓ TV
✓ Tea/Coffee maker   ✓ Fan
✓ Electric kettle
✓ Cable channels
✓ Wardrobe or closet
✓ Upper floors accessible by elevator
✓ Toilet paper

Prices are as per room for 2 nights
Included: Breakfast

A screenshot from Booking.Com with the message
"Only 3 rooms left.." even in the lockdown period

When I ran a search for hotels in Mumbai during lockdown ending on 3rd May, the result still went ahead to convince me that I might lose out on an offer if I do not book NOW!! Here NOW is a situation when all the commercial units are closed in Mumbai.

Forced Continuity

Netflix has undoubtedly hooked consumers to a visually delightful experience. Web series is the trending entertainment for which Netflix comes to rule the market. Netflix offers you a 1-month free subscription and the process is marked by filling a form that not only captures your data but also credit/debit card details. It takes consent from you in fine letters that as soon as the free subscription ends, the next month's subscription fee will be auto-deducted from your account. However, the pattern here is after 1 month you might forget above the auto-debit and one fine day without intimation the fee is debited, even when you didn't want it to.

I recently faced forced continuity under no intimation with Audible App, an audiobooks subscription app.

Roach Motel

The clock is ticking by the second and you are biting your nails as your internet is down and you might just lose out on a dress offer that is about to end in an hour. Are you familiar with such a situation or near around? This is the pattern that misguides consumers by creating an emergency and triggering to buy, even if there was no intention to buy.

A screenshot from Myntra with "Only Few Left!" message

You are in a Roach Motel pattern that has lured you with ease towards great products and exclusive offers and now you are finding it hard to get out of the situation without buying. As a product designer, I have also done a similar messaging for Pepperfry and Peepul Tree, well it was a marketing decision!

Dark Patterns and Trends

EuropeanDataJournalism.Eu offers an interesting statistic of how the different dark patterns play psychologically on consumer behaviour with scarcity topping the charts followed by urgency.

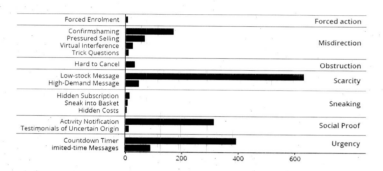

Frequency of dark patterns by category. Source: Dark pattern at scale, findings from a Crawl of 11k shopping websites

How Ethical are Dark Patterns?

Dark patterns are webs that are stealthily laid out to bring promising business to companies, but when questioned in the scope of right practices, it is a dilemma to call dark patterns ethical or unethical.

It is a loud and clear message that dark patterns are dominating us by tricking us in buying or extracting information. However, there are no governing laws or authority that can bring it under the scope of interrogation and bring lawful closures.

The dilemma supports different perspectives for the user and the companies.

User's perspective

For a user, the experience could be one-time or engaging. Companies in the context of comfortable design and accessibility are hooking users to the pattern for comebacks. Faster loading websites, captivating displays, and ease of processing are every user's need and that is what these patterns guarantee.

What might concern a user, in the long run, is data extraction, spamming, paying extra under disguised sales, or loss of reputation. Unless the dark patterns are transparent they are good, but as they get dense, the user behaviours might change the course of the equation, calling it unethical.

Company's perspective

The sales & marketing departments are interested in crunching sales numbers and with the support of the design teams that do a magical job of designing disguised-sales, the dark patterns are marketing gimmicks and very much ethical.

Companies can claim of sharing information, but has the user read it through? Do you remember the- Accept Terms and Conditions checkbox we have all at some time blindly checked? How does someone then go back and claim something that was overlooked?

Dark patterns are technology-backed promotional gimmicks and could be termed as an ethical practice unless a user might begin an ugly charade causing a loss of reputation to the company. Under the immense scope of the business, Dark Patterns create, it is yet a fine line designing companies need to be wary about crossing.

CHAPTER VI

Natural User Experience

A Natural User Experience is a developed system with the motive of human-computer interface and that is built around intuitive human actions that are normal and everyday behaviour to enhance technology. Sometimes these NUI's are seemingly visible for an unhindered experience, whereas in some cases, they are intermediary and responsible for interactions.

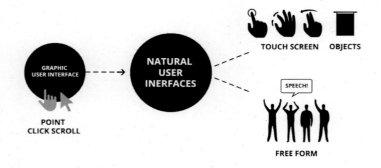

Shifting paradigms

The use of Natural User Interface is not intimidating as they are smartly adapted to natural human behaviour for ease of operations. The Natural User Interface could seek psychology to train if imitating human behaviour in technology had emotions. Yet, the NUI's capture human behaviour such closely that technology is coming to be adapted easily.

Speech, gesture, and voice recognition, touch-controlled systems have been adopted by designers for an unrealistic yet first of its kind experience and the development stays on to build the systems that interact with lesser human effort.

Till some years back only, the UX designers were challenged by visual user interfaces (VUI) and graphics. Our brain responds to different senses varyingly, the vision being the most important sense, followed by smell, taste, sound, and touch. These sensory parameters are explored by designers over the years to present a comfortable experience.

> "*Exploit skills that we have acquired through a lifetime of living in the world, which minimizes the cognitive lead and therefore, minimizes the distraction. Natural User Experiences should always be designed with the use of context in mind.*"

- Bill Buxton, Principal Researcher at Microsoft

Visual interfaces are engaging, but when the need for voice and touch interfaces has to be explored, the technology gets more complex, yet needs to be presented as a simplistic solution. The art is in exploring the nuances of each sensory aspect in detail, the end-user expectations, and the ability to adapt and engage with the latest developments.

This article explores the Touch and Speech aspect of User Interface and how it comes to shape the design for an enhanced experience. Let's explore these two in a bit more details.

Touch

Touch is the prime sensory experience and many developments have been carried around touch senses to influence browsing experiences. The dynamics depend on how people hold their phone, and there are variations as seen in the following figure and data from www.umattres.com/mt/

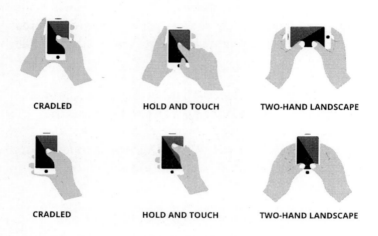

CRADLED   HOLD AND TOUCH   TWO-HAND LANDSCAPE

CRADLED   HOLD AND TOUCH   TWO-HAND LANDSCAPE

Common ways people hold and touch their mobile phone

- 75% of users touch the screen only with one thumb
- Fewer than 50% of users hold their phones with one hand
- 36% of users cradle their phone, using their second hand for both greater reach and stability
- 10% of users hold their phone in one hand and tap with a finger of the other hand

These statistics come to define how the touch-oriented developments come to be adapted in technology.

Interestingly observed that the mobile device screens are seldom touched at the corners or swiped diagonally, while the core of attention is the centre of the screen. This has led to adaptations that designers place important content in the centre of the page and secondary and tertiary date towards the top and bottom.

Voice

Speech recognition has established its mark in technology and making tasks simpler by the mere utterance of a command. Voice commands have come to be part of our life, the AI's await our command and the information is just around. The following image from https://www.toptal.com gives us a clear insight into the way smart speakers are influencing our life and the kind of queries asked.

Use Cases for Smart Speakers:

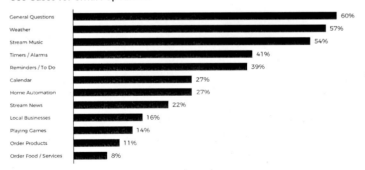

Domains Smart Speakers are used for. Source: Toptal and ComScore

Voice interactions depend largely on connectivity, processing activity, processing speed, applied environment, error in reading, interpretations based on accents to name a few factors. The environment not only means where the technology is applied but also where the technology is practised. While technology applied could be a home or car, where the technology is applied could be indoors or outdoors. The following graph shows a statistic of how people make use of technology in a different environment.

These images give us a glimpse of human-technology interactions in a different environment.

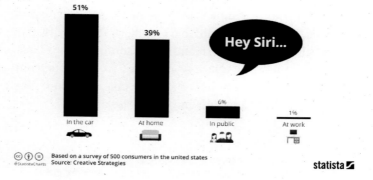

Where people use Voice Assistants

Voice interactions present us different avenues including your Smart TV, Amazon Echo, Smart Thermostat, Google & iPhone assistants to name a few. They are used by organizations for engaging customers for a futuristic experience. Chatbots and Voice Bots are Artificial Intelligence that communicates through textual or speech interactions. Microsoft, Google, Apple, Amazon, and some major companies are already using Voice bots for business interactions and to keep their consumers engaged.

https://industryarc.com states that the voice bot industry is going to see a CAGR growth of 35% between 2018-2023 due to easy accessibility over other apps.

While voice designs are making our tasks easier and manageable, UX designers must identify the kind of gaps in the design and execution models and environmental testing.

Multi-modal Interfaces

Designers have gone to create technological advances that present us the best of all worlds by culminating visual, speech, and touch experiences. Google Maps, is a sensory experience that inculcates both visual, speech, and touch aspects to a defined advantage.

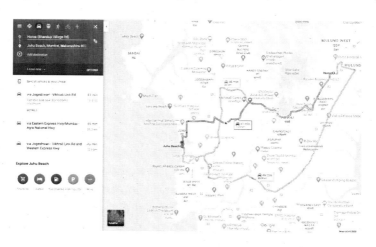

Google Map interface with multiple modals

Self-Driving cars is another multi-modal interface that works around touch, visual, and speech recognition to enhance future technology frontiers.

Interior of a self-driving car

• • •

The Future of Technology is a pleasant experience and inevitable.

The designer can bring an inexplicable experience in technology, however, the transitions from the current to the future have to be done keeping in mind the adapting capacity of the end-users. This means studying and analyzing the learning curve of the end-users, their cognitive acceptance, and their interaction experience with the technology.

From Home entertainment, chatbots, real-time text responders, paired devices, auditory and tactile feedback technology has transitioned and emerged. Designers are exploring the unexperienced domain of gesture recognition, brain-machine interfaces, natural language processing, etc., there is a world to explore, and irreplaceable design to be built.

Touchscreen smartphones were once a fancy, but today a part of every life. Likewise, the adaptation and culmination of experience should be balanced to a product that is promising and well accepted. Technology means ease and creating this ease is a mesh of interfaces and designs; all in the line of enhanced productivity.

CHAPTER VII

Mind Mapping In UX Design

Human brains process images 60,000 times faster than it processes text information. The human brain is wired to communicate better in a visual way. Images have always impacted our long-term memories. Consider an old photo triggering a milieu of emotions and at the same time, an attractive window-shopping display or online shopping window stays put on your memory.

An extension to the imagery learning is seen in the educational system. Images and videos are creating an engaging learning platform, explaining concepts that remain etched in memory. Talking about learning, the concept of mind maps comes to simplify things by learning through pictorial & graphical representations. The concept of Mind maps was first introduced by Tony Buzan (www.TonyBuzan.com) who was a British Psychologist, Educational Consultant, and Author.

Mindmap process

Mind Maps are pictorial or graphical representations that are often very colourful and come to represent educational projects, complex processes, and a tool for brainstorming. Mind maps come to simplify, analyze, organize, and represent processes in a systematic and graphical form.

Mind Maps are but the colourful, imaginative, articulate, multi-dimensional, streamlined flow of ideas that come to form a 2D prototype of the issue at hand.

Mind Maps are very powerful visual mapping strategies for creating detail-oriented and well-articulated process designs. While students use them to memorize concepts, take notes, analyze or prepare presentations, we have seen the use of mind maps in driving complex design work.

UX and UI being design-oriented professions make the use of design, scribbles, graphics, or pictorial representations to brainstorm or present projects. While flow chart is the age-old tool software professionals have grown up with, it has its own restrictions, Concept mapping another tool is used in exhaustive processes and very vast. A concept mapping process can involve mind maps as a category within. Concept maps come with different parent categories whereas mind maps have a single parent category. Another tool designer has been using is the Ontology map, which is branched and specifically connects back and forth and also serves as a connection between two entities. Different tools come to emphasize their individual skills, but mind maps are easy, communicative, and attractive to stay focused and act.

Smashing Magazine states in an article on Design Thinking Process that it involves five stages: empathy, definition, ideation, prototyping, and testing. Designers can easily use mind maps as hierarchical structures to create a clear picture around these five stages.

Why Mind Maps in Design?

Mind Maps make researching easier

Every topic of discussion becomes the parent topic, that bifurcates into different branches of information that comes to define the parent topic. These branches of information can be classified as a source of information, analysis method, data compilation, statistics representation methods, presentation methods, results and conclusions, demographics and sources to publish. Mind maps offer a wide spread of activities in one vision, emphasizing on every aspect that calls for information.

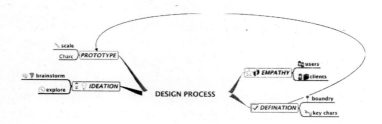

Mindmap in UX design process

Grouping and Sub-grouping

Designers can bifurcate every aspect of the design process into groups and sub-groups. Considering empathy as a parent topic means primarily identifying customer age groups, then branch further to lifestyle, brand preferences, buying patterns, current trends, offers etc.

Buying patterns could also bifurcate further to spending capacity, discounted sale preferences, repetitive site visits and delayed buying, impulsive buying behaviour, random shopping patterns, and all these and many more parameters.

Action-based Commands

Mind maps are not only visual representations of projects but backed by action-based commands to effect action. A good mind map not only lists ideas and end results but the process that can be taken to effect results. Mind maps are therefore action-based and not just pictorial representations.

An app development process would incorporate

Market Survey:

- Run a detailed survey of local as well as national markets to check your App's novelty.
- App users and age groups, phone types- Windows, Android, or iPhone users.
- Current users of a similar existing App etc.

Prototype:

- Authentic design and usability.
- Adaptations – windows, android, and iPhone.
- Design scalability

Such action-based commands can be used in mind maps for clarity of instructions.

Colourful and easy representations

Mind maps are meant to be colourful and attractive to impact results unlike cognitive maps, concept maps or flow charts that basically represent process flows. Mind maps are interactive and engaging wireframes that bring the diverse possibilities of an aspect for wider study and results.

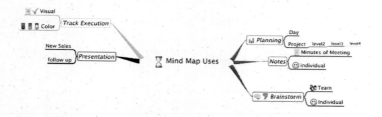

Usage of Mind Map

The cognitive brain understands and responds better to design and pictorial elements to process and remember.

Colourful Artistic Designs Boards to Actual UI designs

Mind maps can be an easy colourful and unusual way to offer client presentations. A UI/UX designer can bring in a detailed map of a UI website that will mark the different pages, page attributes, payment systems, forms, colour themes, templates, back-end/front-end software etc. Imagine such an unusually detailed and attractive presentation will certainly have the client curious for what's in store.

Mind Map as a Brainstorming Tool

The concept of a mind map is a brush that can paint a blank canvas in varied shades. A central and parent topic identified mind maps give you a liberty of thinking in every aspect and direction unlike flow-charts that are dominated with monosyllabic - Yes or No responses.

Mind maps can capture the if's and buts, why and how of an idea and progress it by action-packed process flow.

Adaptations of Mind Maps

Mind maps can be used within the exhaustive Concept Maps to represent Subject-matter or a primary category and its subcategories thereof. Imagine an e-commerce website that is a mesh of interlinked processes and pages. In such designs, mind maps can be incorporated under Concept Maps to associate different parent categories and possible connections.

Mind Map Apps

Although, mind maps bring a sensory pleasure if you are physically preparing them, drawing every object, picking a different colour to identify, differentiate and simplify processes. However, not everyone can bring out creativity and not everyone has the leisure for artistic inclinations. There are some Apps that offer simple to complex mind map templates that you can just feed with inputs.

MindMaster (https://www.edrawsoft.com/mindmaster/) and Lucidchart (https://www.lucidchart.com/pages/examples/mind_mapping_software) are two of the best Mind Mapping Apps in 2020 that are compatible with windows, iOS, Android, and Linux platforms.

Mind maps are organized representations that amplify your ideas and project them in a streamlined process format. If nothing else, mind maps are a visual treat to simplicity that could captivate any designer to start using them.

Special thanks to Mr. Pushkaraj Kolatkar of LearnMindmap for providing the insights and creating all the mindmap illustrations used in this article.

CHAPTER VIII

Why Should A Tech Start-Up Get Their Product Designs Done From a UX Agency?

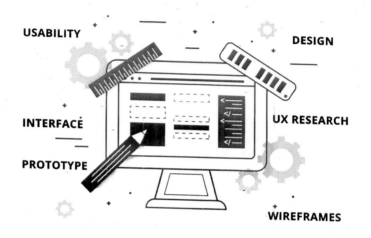

The web and mobile development bandwagon is scaling newer heights with more customers shifting base to the online domain. Even retail outlets have gone online with a distinct promotional strategy of attracting more clients. In the scope of such brimming opportunities and a multitude of possibilities, clients are coming across choosy and informed on creating interactive design aspects. In this scenario, the development companies that bank on their development skills feel the restraint of design-oriented professionals.

Development companies have realised the importance of the design aspect and the specialisation it calls for. The UX team is not only about the look, feel, and usability of design but extends well beyond its scope to undertake research, understand customer engagements, analysing user experiences, and building prototypes that are conveying.

While developers are more of the technical coding league, designers come to enhance aesthetics. Like an architect builds and an interior designer decorates. The tech team might come with strong coding expertise, they will, however, be superficial in the user design aspect. The tech team or the developers are inclined towards the latest technological updates, building backend, support technology and, cloud storage, etc. The UX designers come to fill the need for a comprehensive design that is aesthetically compelling and technically sound.

Tech start-ups who are creating their platforms are looking for creating unforgettable experiences. User design, text, sound, interfaces, and usability are the key elements UX designers came to create. However, these elements are not superficially created to adjust to the different client requirements, but research-oriented strategic planning goes before defining the scope of the project. www.forbes.com states that the number one reason start-ups fail is that they fail to understand, "No Market Need."

While start-ups are all geared up to create experiences that will create a stream of clients, UX designers play an important role in this journey. UX designer has evolved as a profession as well the role quintessentially generates ROI that is the need of every organisation. But primarily, UX designers understand the need of the consumers and

uild it in their products for a satisfactory experience. User
ɔerience is a term common to both the consumer and
client. While the consumer banks on great user
iences for a memorable experience, the client at the
me wants to create such user experience to have
umer come back, we can refer this as customer
ɔ (CX). In this, the common link is the UX
Agency who creates the user experiences.

ɔr Experience is such an important element of
ɔe cycle, it is imperative that the process is
ɔe right finances and timelines. While the
ght understand the need for good design,
lers - the owners or investors might not
he need for good UX expertise. The
in the process need to be convinced
ɔient outcomes User Experience can
ɔrs need to be on the same page as
ing the process.

s, 'According to Analysis 101
ing the users, their needs and
experience is the reason why
ɔs a huge number and can't
show the effect of UX/UI
ɔts to 30% of its success.
f a good business model

thorough customer-
ɔg into the design
multi-faceted role
ɔn or mostly by a

onsumer-
consumers
he market.
will be the
ess involves
ɔf as well as
filled with all
functional to
ites of possible
experience is
ference, goals,
ɔt dynamics all
ɔh. Research on
ɔn with efficient

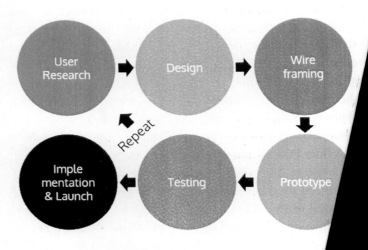

UX process and methodology

Research

The UX researcher conducts concise and ⬚
oriented research for the deep-rooted problems ⬚
are facing with the current similar products in ⬚
Research is carried around the parameters tha⬚
essential elements of the final design. The pro⬚
interviewing sales support and training sta⬚
listening to customer support calls that are ⬚
possible inputs for the system being not⬚
customer expectations. Testing competitor ⬚
design flaws and gaps and ensuring suc⬚
eliminated from the client site. Pr⬚
behaviour, patterns, needs, and mark⬚
broadly form a part of the resear⬚
compatibility, time, and effort reducti⬚

framework suggestions is also the need in place. Research also includes taking feedback on design flows and paper prototypes before advancing to the advancing phase.

Creating Buyer Personas

This is an interesting element of UX designing. Designers create buyer's persona depending on the research analysis. This creates a pool of the predictive consumer base that is going to buy your products and the design team can design around their expectations. This helps streamline processes and efforts.

UX Design

A UX designer based on the research, buyer's persona, and other input at hand come up with a constructive design plan. The UX designer designs wireframes from the research information available. The UX design process begins with idea generation and then refining on that idea. The process includes building frameworks that are structural forms explaining the flow of the ideation.

Visual Design

Visual designers offer muscle to the wireframes with lines, shapes, colours, and textures. They make designs appealing by using the right typography and use of design elements like unity, dominance, scale, contrast, and hierarchy to influence design experiences.

Content Creation & Development

Specific, clear, and fresh content will keep the consumers captivated to your site.

Product Testing

Once the prototype is ready it can be tested for flawless outcomes. User experiences mean smooth and conditioned interactions between the consumers and the system for a comfortable experience.

The content creators and developers work hand-in-hand with the UX team to create the difference. The process should be implemented in line with the above listing. Some stakeholders might drop the research phase, moving directly to the design. They would want the research to be done once prototyping is done. This might then create a set of challenges, making the design team rework on the modules or start fresh killing the time, efforts, and finances involved.

Start-ups do not have the leverage of time and finances and need to act wisely on their spending. UX designers come as a promising choice when designing products because of the comprehensive yet specialised nature of solutions that they can provide.

CHAPTER IX

Designing for the "Gen-Z"

FuturumResearch.Com has coined a very interesting term called Digital Native for the ones born after 2000, the world calls them Generation Z. Adding to Generation Z are the millennials who are not only come to claim the largest share of market products today but, are also will be the next biggest share of the working class. While Generation Z comes totally equipped with mobile and digital media, the millennials are but a mixed lot of digital and analog experiences.

Generation Z is integrally born in the digital wave and does not consider their involvement in the technology as addiction, as the other generations think they are. In fact, Generation Z sees technology as an extension of their normal life. They have aligned and adapted to the technology to fill their social, mental, and physical spaces. The impact of technology so penetrating the lifestyle has its adverse effects and researchers are studying the involvement of Generation Z and their technology involvement.

Gen Z is born to technology and they see technology as inseparable. Rather their smartphone devices are such an integral part of their lifestyles that it resembles an extended organ of their body. Education, entertainment, shopping, ordering food, booking movie tickets, or online banking, everything is at their fingertips. Gen Z is spoilt for information and choices and therefore they value technology as a practical tool and not a developmental luxury. While the other generations have come a long way adopting and adjusting to technology, Gen Z is riding the technology wave. No wonder you see babies, surfing YouTube for their favourite rhymes and children gamming like professionals. The adult Gen Z is supported to deal with different challenges except for the emotional one through technology. For emotional ones too they can easily reach their friends through technology.

The traditional shift to marketing and buying patterns:

The buying patterns for Generation Z has largely been the digital way. The millennials and now the Generation Z are posing a challenge to marketers and promoters to hook these young consumers to screen. Considering the very short attention span and multiple screen juggling practices. The challenge is to keep these young consumers glued to your screen. Short and crisp is the way ahead for Generation Z.

The Budding Clients:

It will not be a distant day when Gen Z will be the major clientele. From schoolwork, games, surfing, texting, shopping, and entertainment, Gen Z relies on technology. Going forth many applications and products need to be designed around the needs of Gen Z. To capture this wave of Gen Z in all its fervour, designers and companies need to be workaround a few parameters that will define the user experiences for Gen Z.

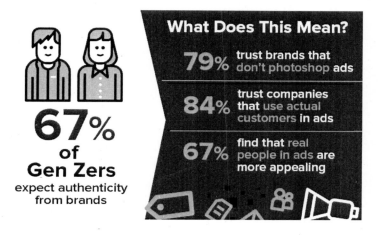

Image by FinancesOnline with data sources from
CNBC, Ad Age, and Forbes

Dependence on Memory:

Generation Z and to an extent the millennials are up for easy grabs for a calculator for solving simple math. The dependence on scheduler apps for updates and reminders is common. They have glued on to the screen and adrift from the world under the veil of their headphones. The short-term memory dependency of Generation Z is dependent and supported and controlled by the scheduler. They are continuously fed with a sea of data and thus a limitation to remember, recollect and the process is left to the comfort of external devices and technology.

Forbes.Com states, we off-load memories to 'the cloud' just as readily as we would to a family member, friend, or lover. It may be that the Internet is taking the place not just of other people as external sources of memory but also of our own cognitive facilities. The researchers call it "the

Google effect."

Attention Span:

The plethora of information makes data accessibility so easy that the essential what? and why? is often lost in a flood of information. The attention span of Generation Z is just 8 secs and they browse a minimum of 5 screens at a time.

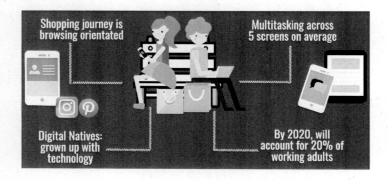

Zen-G in Retail, image by OpenBusinessCouncil.Org

Influencers to Marketers:

Generation Z is not celebrity endorsement kinds. They are the ones who are captivated by the maximum follower bases- the influencers. YouTube has therefore seen the most subscriber base as Generation Z. The belief in what the masses believe, then call it herd mentality or a choice.

Working Designs:

Designs that are bold, captivating, and trendy will catch the fancy of a Gen Z, but be wary that their attention span is a few seconds and to make them stay on your product site is to supplement them with valuable information and insights, leading to call for action.

Building Content:

Gen Z would go through as much information to get their desired inputs. But, if you want to anchor the Gen Z to your product, creating compelling, authentic, and versatile content is the need.

Fluid Borders:

Geographical barriers are not a concern of Gen Z. For them, this world is their playground. Gen Z is easily accessible to information across the world and that has again changed their decision-making power. The comparison now is not locally, but internationally. The fluid geographical borders technology presents have made Gen Z more worldly and accepting. Their tastes and communication sphere has enhanced to worldwide options. Worldwide education prospects and online shopping are the majorly accessed options.

Gen Z calls for constant information and likes to regale in this whirlwind of information. They are spoilt for choice and are experimental with their outlook.

There is a sea change the generations over the last decades have transitioned over. Lifestyles, education patterns, travel, food, culture, and business have all influenced under the scope of technology. However, as Gen X or Gen Y, who were adroitly sharp at their memory and remember facts and figures from the wee days, are the Millennials and Gen Z losing the power of memory over cloud-based artificial storages as well as smartphone devices. The transition is to a technology-based lifestyle that is facilitating, yet, daunting the mere existence of your inherent resources. Call it development or name it an addiction, the fact is, the world is changing and so are the behavioural patterns.

Going forth, the challenge is not to deviate the Gen Z from technology, but be able to build experiences that are making Gen Z spend more and valuable time on your product page. The earlier generations would call this paradigm shift merely losing control to technology whereas, the Gen Z calls it 'Tuned-in to Technology.'

CHAPTER X

How Users Get Motivated Towards Using Some Apps Due To The Disastrous Situation?

(Disclaimer: The apps mentioned here, I am neither promoting them nor attached with them anyway nor designed any of them, I noticed the usage of these in recent past and using their names so the reader can easily understand)

In these looming times of lockdown distress, the one apparent hope people have is their smartphone. The once luxury or entertaining device smartphone is today a lifeline to people. Today, the thin line between apprehension and comfort has been crossed; and consumers have come to the big and fascinating world of utilising mobile apps extensively. Call it the situational need, but once you are hooked to a mobile app and its comfort and utility, there is a grim chance of withdrawing.

While some mobile apps are pre-installed to all the smartphones, the ones that you will download are primarily for utility and secondarily for entertainment. Mobile Apps that have been existent for some time have been accepted under the crucial challenges of time and accessibility.

When demonetization was announced in India back in 2017, the entire Indian fraternity was taken by a storm. Cashless transactions were the only option, as the old currency was void. As stated by the Times of India, 'the government's move of demonetization has driven people to go cashless and depend on mobile apps.'

69

BHIM

The BHIM App is another indigenous app developed to help the cashless crises of demonetization. The app was launched by the Prime Minister of India, 2 months after the demonetization in Nov 2017. Players like Paytm, a mobile wallet company had a crucial role to play during the cashless times of demonetization. Paytm, is India's largest mobile payment wallet company with more than 100 million users and more than 2 million transactions per day. Within 2 days of the Indian Government's move to demonetize, the app saw a considerable surge of 3 times the app download, as well as 5 times offline transactions moving to online. According to www.moneycontrol.com, the company saw a monumental user base increase from 140 million in October 2016 to 270 million in November 2017. Additionally, the company's merchant base has swollen to 5 million from 8,00,000 in 2016.

Today, the PayTM app sits comfortably in your smartphone as a crucial money transaction app. The transactions being carried out by merely a couple of clicks. Apps are built around our comfort, but we have to adapt them and utilise. Many brilliant utility-based apps come to promise convenience and time management. At the same time, they can track and document details for easy use in the recurrent transactions.

In recent times of Covid-19, the corporate culture has shifted temporarily where the business operating modules are driven by video chats. The need of the time is communicating and to keep business going. The social distancing norms and stay safe indoor slogans have made us rely to a great extent on video calling apps. Statista.Com highlights the whopping trend of how people have shifted to the video calling domain to keep businesses going. Zoom calls lead the charts with Skype following suit. Skype however still leads with the number of daily active users. Video calls have made business convenient. Not only saving time but essentially meeting the current need to communicate. Video chats are a window to the world in these grim times.

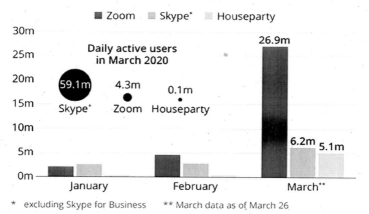

Video Chat Apps Rise to Prominence Amid Pandemic

Global downloads of video chat apps for Android and iOS

Image source Statista, research data by PrioriData

It is not a fancy that we are facing a second historic moment in the last 3 years, demonetization and now Covid-19. In these difficult times of low accessibility of cash and physical operations, mobile apps have come to support us in every possible way. Grocery, electronics, books, clothes, cakes, flowers, medicines, and hardware, you name anything and the mobile apps can source it for you. At the forefront of COVID-19, gaming apps and tik-tok have experienced the maximum downloads.

Source Acko.Com

Arogya Setu App

The Arogya Setu App has considerably crossed a download of 50 Million and is an indigenous app to India. The Arogya Setu App was launched by the Ministry of Health to efficiently track and update on the COVID-19 situation. The App received a whopping download post the Prime Minister Narendra Modi's mention about it in his Nationwide speech on April'14.

App Name	1 Mar - 11 Mar, 2020	11 Mar - 25 Mar, 2020	25 Mar - 10 Apr, 2020
Tiktok	10,300,000	18,900,000	14,100,000
WhatsApp	12,600,000	11,200,000	6,800,000
Zoom	125,000	3,600,000	14,500,000
Vigo	1,200,000	1,400,000	1,400,000
Helo	6,300,000	7,300,000	8,400,000
Telegram	1,100,000	1,900,000	3,600,000
ShareChat	1,100,000	1,600,000	2,000,000
PubG	3,200,000	5,000,000	5,300,000
Tinder	240,000	361,000	336,000
Bigo Live	743,000	1,100,000	1,400,000
Likee	2,500,000	3,400,000	3,800,000
Ludo King	3,700,000	6,700,000	9,500,000
Houseparty	5,000	335,000	1,500,000

Most Downloaded Apps in India in March and April
2020. Source: Sensor Tower

*"New app downloads on Android and iOS stood at
22 billion and nine billion respectively. Non-gaming
apps accounted for 55 percent of overall downloads
on Google Play Store, and 65 percent on Apple App
Store."*

- YourStory.Com

The App industry is competitive and preference driven.
Yet, the usability factor and technical support is the prime
element that drives downloads.

The next important element that drives consumers
towards downloads is value-added services. The current
COVID-19 situation has rendered people to their homes,
accessibility is limited, and, in such times, how mobile app
companies can come to make a difference? Technology
supported by the human factor goes a long mile in
establishing relations. Mobile app companies like Swiggy

and Zomato have initiated the deliveries with preset information about the chef's body temperature and that of the delivery person.

Livemint.Com, in one of its latest news, brings forth the essential cross-brand associations to service consumers. Nivea India, in a bid to service its clients with essential hygiene products during the COVID-19 lockdown situation, has tied-up with Zomato and Swiggy for deliveries within 60 to 90 minutes within a city. Domino's Pizza and ITC have also associated to deliver ITC's essential products like wheat flour and spices.

Mobile app companies are building convenient experiences around health, entertainment, pharmacy, and convenience items. Brands are bringing an advantage to their consumers by acting as extensions to their needs. The effort is human and back-end technology. While situations will not remain the same and consumers might soon return to retail shopping; mobile apps will still rule the game with the convenience and easy access they bring to the trade.

CHAPTER XI

The UX Design Trends – 2010-2020

User experiences have been shifting to newer paradigms to cater to consumer preferences and to emerge as market leaders. Initiating a new trend means a pivotal experience, and testing that, gauges how consumers are adapting to the newer trends. While technology can never be underrated and stabilized, innovative design experiences are the need for changing times. Let us see here how newer trends have in the last decade has been a contributor to the design experiences.

From Click to Touch Experiences

Moving largely from the big desktop screens to the smaller and palm compatible smartphones, a major consumer shift has driven the industry in the last decade. While desktop-based software solutions might be an investment in the decade 2000-2010, the last decade has majorly moved to the smartphone interface. The design experiences have transitioned largely from the click of a mouse to touch. Not only this but the exponential rise in smartphone usage has urged companies to consider their investments from web-based to mobile-based applications. While work operations are still largely controlled by the desktop-based application, product sales and promotions are making use of smartphones to anchor consumers. An easy, on the go touch and shop experience, is like a magic wand solution the design experience has created in the last decade.

Single and Social Login Across Apps

With the plethora of mobile apps, and their unique features and solutions, smartphones are populated with hordes of applications. However, with every app remembering the login and password details remain a challenge. Creating login information for every app and then remembering all the necessary logins is a task. The omnipresent apps like Facebook and Google have come to rescue by offering a common login option across different apps and platforms. Now this seems like a comfortable solution, but as a consumer, I am sharing my Facebook login, my phone gallery and GPS location, and many more mandatory details asked by different apps under the pretense of a comfortable one-click log in. Does that sound developed and secure?

There are companies that are offering a one password service across all your passwords. Companies like Onelogin offer a master password solution for your different login needs.

Biometrics

What came as a comfort in this decade, is a solution, that is beyond sharing data and remembering multiple passwords and uniquely specific to an individual. Adopting biometric technology to log in a device has largely brought a new dimension to the security solutions. Fingerprints and facial detection have been a new way to log in.

Website vs. Social Media

Get a company website!! Where would your clients find you otherwise? In this decade, the trend has largely shifted, with companies merely creating websites to park their information, while moving their sales, promotions, and branding activities to social platforms. The social platforms come with an already existing online population and that makes work easier. The transition of business communities to an online social networking platform has been another prominent trend the current decade has experienced. Social Media is also now the new business marketing community platform.

White Space

The homepage of ONYX design, where I kept 90% whitespace

Minimalist is sophisticated, clear, and concise. There has been a shift in trend from design-heavy websites to the clutter-free and more white spaces. Flaunting white space in design is a bold step and needs clarity of thought, design, and implementation. White spaces command attention, the minimalist design has to be boldly expressive to balance the large white spaces.

Drop the Menu

How long would they cascade? The painstaking drop-down menus have finally been a design trend of the past and websites are appearing clean and smooth on design and functionality. The maze of pages that sit in menus one below the other is a nightmare that was still more accessible on desktop but became challenging with smartphones. The design trends have over the decade adapted to the mobile platform. Websites today are compatible across web and mobile interface and hence have shed the drop-down menus to engage design usability as well as functional comfort.

Transparency in Design

Dark patterns are a solution that has been extensively used in the last decade to influence consumers towards a call for action. The underlying design behind the dark patterns are basically misleading and have been conflicting on the ethical principles of companies. While dark patterns make appear designs simplistic, they are inconspicuous to the layman and leading to bigger and deeper design manipulation.

Brands are misinforming, and this to a larger extent leaves the consumer in a state of ambiguity. The line between facts and factual misrepresentations has to be a conscious ethical parameter design company should consider. Fake followers, fake credentials, fake customer reviews, and testimonials are all ruling the market and question the very existence of authenticity.

Dark Pattern – Roach Motel, Source Dylan Thomas

While the disturbing dark patterns are an adapted business strategy for many companies, going forth what needs to be accepted are stronger principles and ethical practices in business. Designs should be created to make solutions more usable, functional, and attractive and not to mislead.

Custom Mobile Apps

Businesses have over the last decade adapted to custom-made mobile applications that are business-specific and customer-driven. Companies are creating a user experience that is handy and do not require efforts. The comfort of accessing a service is now merely at the touch of a screen. This endeavor has been towards providing value-added solutions to clients and at the same time maintaining customer patronage.

Conversational Mediums

Consumer communication pattern has shifted over the years from online customer support to pre-recorded, task-based calls, or case-specifics queries addressed by chatbots. While chatbots are adopted by many companies to replace the costlier expense of maintaining a physical staff, they are yet groping for customer attention. Consumers too are transitioning from the idea of a live support call to an AI-based support system. Personal communication yet rules the game, in understanding customer emotions that drive decisions.

Screenshot of the AI-based Chatbot from ONYX UX Studio website where the bot asks the user a set of questions

The Antidote

While companies that created image editing software are now creating an interface that can identify a morphed image against the original one. Voice, image, and content plagiarism has circulated a sea of adulterated content that is misinforming and misleading. Companies that initiated image editing software like Adobe, is now coming with an antidote that can through AI track image and voice morphing.

The need for design will be a perpetual one, but understanding the current trends and consumer preferences, how companies are balancing their design for affecting sales vs sustenance is to be seen in the coming times.

CHAPTER XII

Customer Experience Trends 2020

Consumer experiences define the future of businesses. What consumers contribute to the business is a major stake. Consumers come to buy your ideologies, they come to live the dream products or services that you have created for them.

Customers Push Companies to Do Better

■ Consumers ■ Business Buyers

80% of customers say the experience a company provides is as important as its products and services

95% of customers say they are more likely to be loyal to a company they trust

67% of customers say their standard for good experiences are higher than ever

Source: MadMe

In such a scenario, consumers are the live-wire that regulates your business and could propel it or disintegrate. However, there are competitors who might be offering similar products and services, how are you different in retaining your customers or creating unique consumer experiences that make them your patrons? We have encountered the trends in technology, promotions, and market variations. The fact is, companies have very recently been receptive and sensitive about the human factor. They have been considering the human element in the entire game right from design, execution, feedback, and redesign. Consumer experiences are all about that and we will be seeing some trends that have been the highlights of the decade between 2011-2020.

Video Marketing:

The marketing world has realigned itself to motion promotion. A distinct jump from the textual and visual stills to video interactions that are captivating and enriching consumers. Video marketing has made browsing interesting and informative. Integrating promotional or informational videos on your website, apps or social media platform has brought a considerable transformation in customer engagement and output.

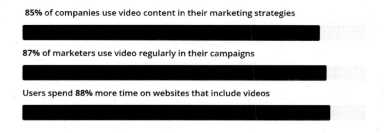

85% of companies use video content in their marketing strategies

87% of marketers use video regularly in their campaigns

Users spend 88% more time on websites that include videos

Image by Devrix

Video chats are also another effective medium to converse and interact with consumers in a real-time sense offering faster solutions and retaining customers.

The Omnipresent Entity:

Targeting one medium of promotion and sitting back comfortably does not serve the purpose today. Like when you fish in an ocean you have a sea of options, then why stick to one? Creating a platform for promotions that can be used across channels and mediums. As the Digital Marketing Experts say, you don't know where does your next client might come from? Being omnipresent is being available on different social media platforms, then you be available in the video media format or your regular content, but be visible and grab the limelight.

You have to document where your earlier customers have come from and where there is potential for attracting your prospective customers. You have to plan a journey across various channels having known your existing consumer trails and accordingly go and set strategies for offering consumer experiences that are unique. Ensure a consistent journey that ensures your consumer loyalty.

Robotic Process Automation:

What progresses in a repeat mode can be automated and we have already used technology to assist us. Adapting to Robotic processes means easing the physical turmoil towards a time-saving and effective solution.

RPA ensures a clear roadmap that is defined around project expectations, setting timelines, approach, and mechanisms, and play in repeat mode for scaled-up experiences.

Augmented Reality:

With google catching our attention with the augmented 3D animals at the start of the lockdown series worldwide, under the COVID-19 situation, augmented reality is not just restricted to entertainment but goes much beyond to business and enhanced consumer engagement.

Nintendo's Pokémon searching app has been a worldwide craze and much adapted because of its near reality interface. Likewise, the US Army has built a Tactical Augmented Reality for Enhanced Situational Awareness and easy maneuvering (https://www.adobe.com/in/insights/5-realworld-examples-of-augmented-reality-innovation.html).

Augmented Reality finds a lot of practical implementations as it presents a near reality situation and lets one envision on the output. Many product-based companies have switched to augmented reality to bring a dynamically engaging interface that can make consumers sensitized towards a quick call for action.

THE IMPACT OF AUGMENTED REALITY ON RETAIL

40%
would be willing to pay more for a product if they could experience it through augmented reality

61%
of shoppers prefer to shop at stores that offer augmented reality, over ones that don't

71%
of shoppers would shop at a retailer more often if they offered augmented reality

The impact of AR on retail, source: Space Technologies

Many product-based companies that have adapted to augmented reality have lesser customer complaints as well as fewer product returns.

Augmented reality is also used to conduct training across geographical diversity.

Mobile Apps:

Companies have gone to the extent of creating exclusive apps for customers for value-added services. These apps present activities well beyond sales and promotions, where the customer interest is purely captured and supplemented under customer engagement activities and loyalty programs.

Data Protection:

While the customer engagements are moving online, there is a sea of sensitive data that is transacted, and to retain the best interest of the consumers, a robust security system has been the overwhelming need. To capture data and to protect it, calls for expert data security solutions. A single data leak case or a dissatisfied client can be a blow to the company's image and in effect can cause an avalanche of concerns once this dissatisfied customer reaches social media.

Transparency:

Companies should not only ensure enhanced data protection solutions but also maintain transparency measures on sharing information. In lieu of the company's philosophies and ethical practices, clear communication should be maintained across information shared including the pricing, offers, and business practices. This way the consumers can relate to your brand philosophy and will certainly indulge in patronage.

Predictive Analysis:

While research and findings have been the trend of decades where marketing professionals have been banking on analyzed data to deduce upcoming promotional strategies. Predictive analysis is more so real-time data analytics that works around the consumer journey, buying patterns, spending patterns, time spent on the website, and different platforms the brand is promoting on. The predictive analysis can help to define and optimising marketing campaigns as well as maintain the right inventory and resources.

Mobile First

The entire technology bandwagon has shifted from the

desktop to the mobile interface. Companies are interested in captivating the audience through the mobile medium as smartphones have been a constant companion and easily accessible to the consumers.

Voice Control:

The voice control technique has been largely adopted in the last decade. From the physical workforce to voice-enabled customer support, the trends have changed in the last decade. Automated voice-based calls that drive towards time-saving mechanisms and effectively handled customer complaints also come as a cost-saving measure.

The entire intention behind these different consumer experience trends has been towards capturing individual customer attention in building a system that not only delivers ongoing sales but also engages consumers in brand patronage. The idea is going for consumer-specific requirements and tapping customer feedback and unsolved requests towards a way to build proactive systems that deliver as per the consumer preferences.

Thank You

A big thank you from me for spending your time and reading the articles, I would love to hear from you what you feel about the book, you may leave your feedback on the online platforms from where you purchased the book from, or send me an email directly to amolendu.h@onyxdigi.com.

I keep posting my articles on Linkedin and you may connect or follow me at https://www.linkedin.com/in/amolenduh/ or see more about my UX Studio at www.onyxdigi.com.

Thank you again.

Amolendu H.